AMAZING RESCUE VEHICLES
FIRE TRUCKS

BY LORI DITTMER

CREATIVE EDUCATION • CREATIVE PAPERBACKS

Published by Creative Education and Creative Paperbacks
P.O. Box 227, Mankato, Minnesota 56002
Creative Education and Creative Paperbacks are imprints of
The Creative Company
www.thecreativecompany.us

Design by The Design Lab
Production by Dana Cheit
Art direction by Rita Marshall
Printed in the United States of America

Photographs by Alamy (ZUMA Press, Inc.), Dreamstime (Ulrich
Mueller), iStockphoto (400tmax, Avatar_023, benoitb, Marc
Dufresne, FrankvandenBergh, KarenHBlack, MattGush, mizoula,
NickS, palinchakjr, ryasick, tazytaz, VCNW)

Library of Congress Cataloging-in- Publication Data
Names: Dittmer, Lori, author.
Title: Fire trucks / Lori Dittmer.
Series: Amazing rescue vehicles.
Includes bibliographical references and index.
Summary: A basic exploration of the parts, equipment, and
variations of fire trucks, the firefighting rescue vehicles. Also
included is a pictorial diagram of the important rescue vehicle and
its equipment.
Identifiers: ISBN 978-1-64026-042-9 (hardcover) / ISBN 978-1-
62832-630-7 (pbk) / ISBN 978-1-64000-158-9 (eBook)
This title has been submitted for CIP processing under LCCN
2018938943.

CCSS: RI.1.1, 2, 4, 5, 6, 7; RI.2.2, 5, 6, 7, 10; RI.3.1, 5, 7, 8;
RF.1.1, 3, 4; RF.2.3, 4

First Edition HC 9 8 7 6 5 4 3 2 1
First Edition PBK 9 8 7 6 5 4 3 2 1

Table of Contents

Fire trucks are rescue vehicles. They help people escape burning buildings and cars. They put out fires. Early fire trucks were water tanks pulled by horses. People pumped the water by hand.

Fire stations once housed horses. Now trucks park in the garage.

Drivers pull over to the side of the road to let fire trucks pass.

Today's fire trucks are powered by machines. The trucks leave the fire station in a hurry. They turn on flashing lights and **sirens**. These warn people to stay out of the way.

sirens warning devices that make long, loud noises

Firefighters may cut a hole in the roof to let out heat and smoke.

A ladder truck carries ladders and other tools to help firefighters get into buildings. This truck has a **turntable** ladder on top. It can reach tall buildings.

turntable a circular platform that can turn around

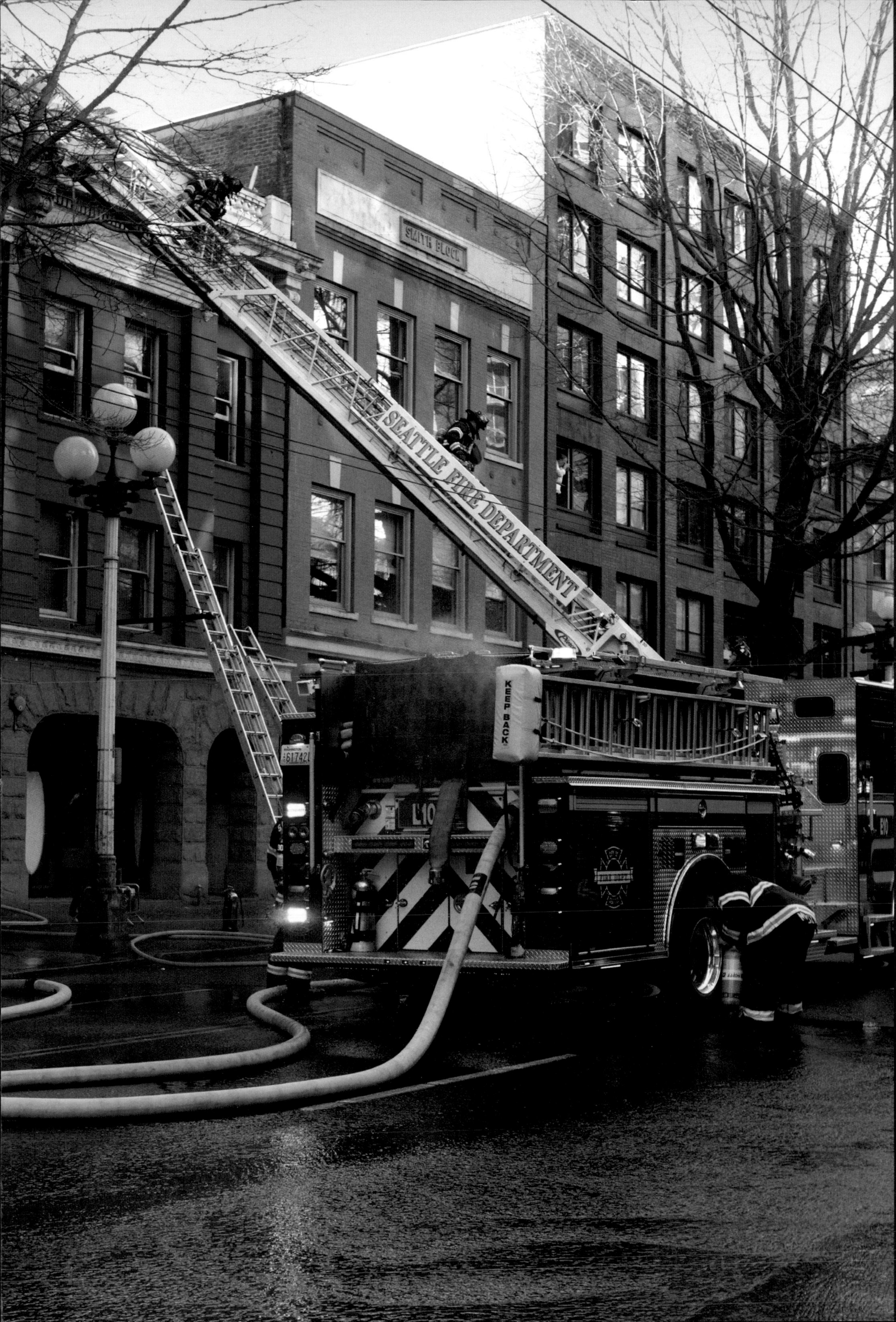
SMITH BLOCK
SEATTLE FIRE DEPARTMENT
KEEP BACK
L10

A fire truck's water tank holds about 1,000 gallons (3,785 l).

A fire engine is also called a pumper. It has a water tank and fire hoses. It can spray water until firefighters connect to a **hydrant**.

hydrant an upright water pipe that can be connected to a fire hose

In an **emergency**, people in the United States call 911. **Dispatchers** answer the call. They tell firefighters where to go.

dispatchers people who receive messages and quickly send emergency services where they are needed

emergency an unexpected, dangerous situation that requires immediate action

A *firefighter's gear typically weighs more than 50 pounds (22.7 kg).*

Firefighters ride

in fire trucks. They wear helmets and fireproof clothing. This helps protect them. Firefighters carry **fire extinguishers** and tools to get into buildings.

fire extinguishers small tanks that spray foam, gas, or other materials to put out fires

Brush trucks fight grass fires. They drive to areas that larger engines cannot reach. They pump water while they drive. Quints can do five jobs. They have a pump, water tank, hoses, ladders, and a turntable ladder. Tankers carry water to places that might not have a hydrant nearby.

Brush fires are hard to put out when it is hot and dry.

Firefighters keep their trucks clean and ready to go. They talk to dispatchers on a two-way radio. They rush to accidents and fires. They help in places where dangerous liquids have spilled.

Firefighters may close off the area around a spill to keep people safe.

Fire trucks fight fires. They save lives. The next time you see one, try to figure out which kind it is. Think about the amazing work it is doing!

Fire trucks and other rescue vehicles rush to emergencies to help people.

Fire Truck Blueprint

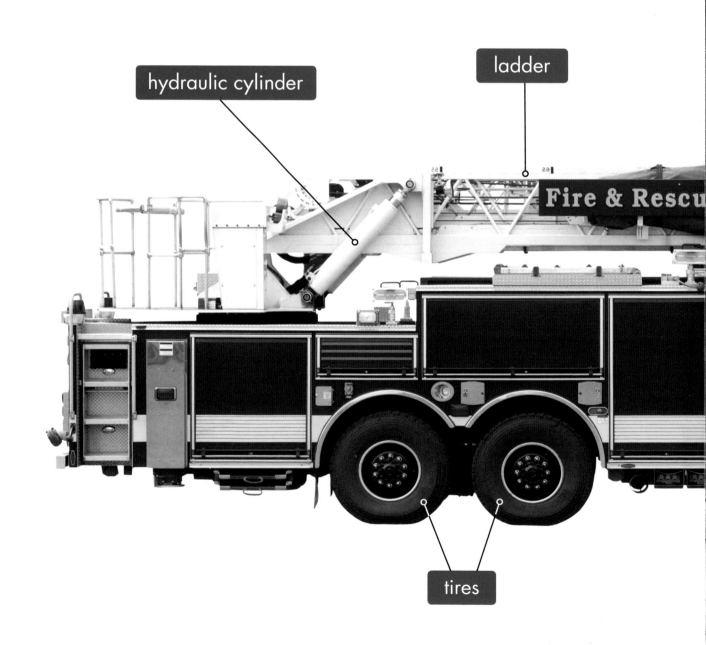

hydraulic cylinder

ladder

Fire & Rescu

tires

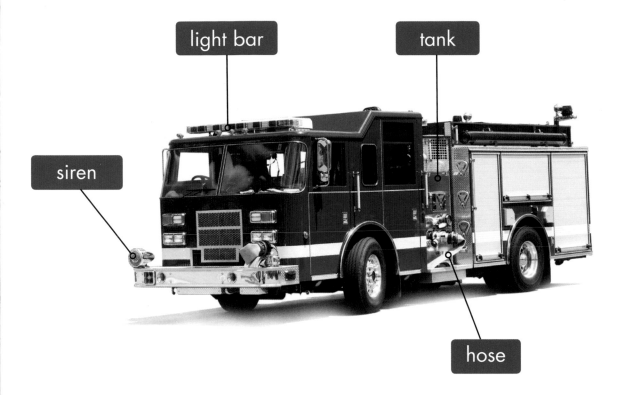

light bar

tank

siren

hose

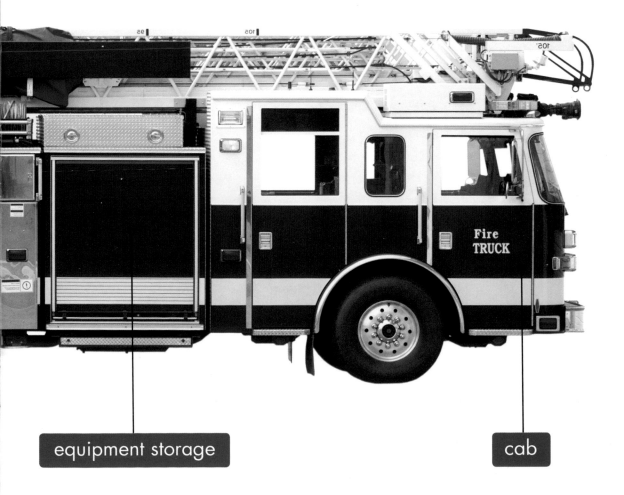

equipment storage

cab

Read More

Bowman, Chris. *Fire Trucks*. Minneapolis: Bellwether Media, 2017.

Fortuna, Lois. *Fire Trucks*. New York: Gareth Stevens, 2017.

Websites

Fire Safe Kids
http://www.firesafekids.org
Read about fire safety, play online games, and print out a picture to color.

National Fire Protection Association: Sparky
http://www.sparky.org
Learn about the parts of a fire truck, watch videos, and print out activity pages.

Note: Every effort has been made to ensure that the websites listed above are suitable for children, that they have educational value, and that they contain no inappropriate material. However, because of the nature of the Internet, it is impossible to guarantee that these sites will remain active indefinitely or that their contents will not be altered.

Index